THE LITTLE BOOK OF

JANE AUSTEN

Written by Emily Wollaston

THE LITTLE BOOK OF

JANE AUSTEN

This edition first published in the UK in 2008
By Green Umbrella Publishing

© Green Umbrella Publishing 2008

www.gupublishing.co.uk

Publishers Jules Gammond and Vanessa Gardner

Printed and bound in China

ISBN 978-1-906229-58-0

Contents

Introduction   4

Chapter 1
Austen Country   20

Chapter 2
The Novels   30

Chapter 3
Film and Television   72

Chapter 4
Celebrating Jane Austen   80

Chapter 5
The Jane Austen Society   90

Introduction

Often revered for being the first writer to give the novel its modern day character, Jane Austen was widely read during her own lifetime, even though her books were published anonymously. With just six major titles such as *Sense And Sensibility, Pride And Prejudice, Mansfield Park, Emma, Persuasion* and *Northanger Abbey,* Austen, who began her writing career in order to entertain her family, was set to become one of the greatest all time classical authors.

Jane's father, the Reverend George Austen, was born in 1731. His mother died in childbirth and her son was sent to live with his aunt in Tonbridge, Kent, when his father died a year after marrying for the second time. His stepmother did not want the responsibility of her husband's offspring and the undoubtedly handsome young man earned a Fellowship to study at St John's Oxford where he also worked as assistant chaplain and dean of arts. His time at Oxford University saw George Austen receive a Batchelor of Arts, a Master of Arts and a Bachelor of Divinity degree, as well as working as a lecturer in Greek. The quiet and scholarly George Austen met Cassandra Leigh, who was born in 1739, when she visited her uncle in Oxford. It is strongly suggested, by documents written at the time, that Austen was very much in love with his witty and lively wife, who upon marriage to the Reverend, ran an economical yet comfortable household. The couple would have eight children (six sons and two daughters) who miraculously all survived into

LEFT An original family portrait of English novelist Jane Austen

CLASSIC LITERATURE

RIGHT Steventon, the birthplace of Jane Austen

adulthood. It is known through Jane's letters to her family members that she enjoyed a happy childhood where she was well loved and cared for.

Jane, born in 1775, was the Austen's second daughter and the seventh of the eight children. James (1765-1819) was the oldest of the Austen siblings and was scholarly like his father. He left for Oxford University at the age of 14 in 1779 and was ordained as a clergyman in 1787. George Austen (1766-1838) named for his father, suffered developmental disabilities and possibly profound deafness and was confined to living in care for his entire life. Edward (1767-1852) had a head for business and, having been adopted by Thomas and Catherine Knight (extremely rich cousins of the Austen family) in the early 1780s, experienced the "Grand Tour" – where rich young men travelled around Europe – before inheriting his adoptive family's estate whereupon he took their family name.

Henry Austen was born in 1771 and like his mother was witty and charismatic. He became Jane's favourite brother, despite his failed ventures (he suffered bankruptcy in 1815) and died some 33 years after his famous younger sister. The next child born to George and Cassandra Austen was their first daughter, Cassandra Elizabeth (1773-1845), who was Jane's most constant companion and true confident. This fact has been shown through the 100 or so surviving letters sent by Jane to her only sister. Cassandra, however, destroyed many of the letters she received from Jane in the years following the young author's death. Frank (1774-1865) and Charles (1779-1852) joined the Royal Navy when both brothers reached the age of 12 (both were based in Portsmouth) and subsequently went on to become Admirals after fighting in the Napoleonic wars.

Born in Steventon, near Basingstoke, on 16 December, Jane spent the first 25 years of her life in Hampshire where she was mainly tutored at home. She did, however, attend school on an occasional basis and was lucky in that her education was much broader than that of her peers. Her aptitude for writing led to her entertaining her large family with her musings and literature and both her parents were avid readers (despite the fact that reading novels was considered a questionable activity at the time). Her earliest writings date from about 1787 (when she was around 12 years old) but Jane was renowned for being shy about her work. The author worked on small pieces of paper which she would hide quickly and discreetly should visitors come to the rectory. Later in life, a creaking door remained unfixed so that she could hear approaching visitors and it gave just enough time for the novelist to hide her work. Her early writings were observant and chatty and she was supported whole-heartedly by her parents who encouraged their young daughter's aspirations. They bought Jane paper and a writing desk and even tried to help get her work published; *First Impressions* (later entitled *Pride And Prejudice*) would be the first novel offered for publication.

As Jane grew and matured into a young woman, she socialised with the upper middle classes and rich landed gentry whom she came to portray in satire in her novels. Her outlook was further broadened by the numerous relatives and friends with whom she spent her time and it became commonplace with the Austen family to put on amateur theatricals. Between 1782 and 1784 the family put on plays at the Steventon rectory and three years later had advanced to more elaborate productions which were mainly put on in the barn located to the side of the family home.

Jane continued to read extensively and critically and this led to her first juvenilia which included comic and amusing pieces on parodies and variations of 18th century literature in both novel and serious history formats. By the age of 23, Jane had written three novels: *Elinor And Mariane,* an early version of *Sense And Sensibility* (1811), *First Impressions,* which was later to transpire as *Pride And Prejudice* (1813) and *Susan,* the early version of *Northanger Abbey* (1818). *First Impressions* was offered to a publisher by George Austen but they declined to even look at the manuscript.

With a fairly good income of around £600 a year, George Austen was by no means rich, (he had eight children to support) but his wife and children lived a comfortable existence which was supplemented by tutoring pupils who came to live with the family while they were studying. In 1783, Cassandra and Jane were sent to Mrs Cawley in Oxford and later Southampton to further their education. An infectious disease at the school saw both girls brought home before they then attended Abbey boarding school in Reading. Back at home – where the majority of their tutoring took place – the two sisters were taught music (piano) and drawing, but the Reverend Austen's extensive library of 500 books gave Jane the foundation she desired and satisfied her thirst for knowledge.

Jane's life consisted of learning and social events including dances and parties (which she particularly enjoyed), but she also loved visits to London, Bath and Southampton where she would attend concerts and watch plays. Although Jane never married, she had a mutual flirtation with Thomas Lefroy, a relative of Mrs Anne Lefroy, one of the author's close friends between 1795 and 1796. Anne Lefroy wasn't particularly enamoured with the relationship – Lefroy, who eventually became Chief Justice of Ireland, couldn't afford to marry Jane – and tried to interest her in the Reverend Samuel Blackall, but the young writer was less than impressed. Jane was even less impressed when her father decided to retire and take his family to Bath in late 1800. The family moved in 1801 and each summer would visit the seaside for a family holiday.

It was on one of these holidays that Jane met a young suitor (whom her sister Cassandra thought would be appropriate for her), but before the young couple could formalise their union, the family were advised of his premature death. The only evidence there is to give credence to this story is in the letters that Cassandra wrote to various nieces after Jane's death. Jane was 27 at the time of the liaison. It is not known whether this experience was portrayed in *Persuasion* (1817). This brief encounter was followed by a proposal from Harris Bigg-Wither, the 21-year-old son of the Bigg family from Manydown, near Steventon. Jane is known to have accepted the proposal, even though she was not in love with Bigg-Wither, but retracted her agreement the following day. Despite the fact that it caused some social

ABOVE 4 Sydney Place, the Bath residence of Jane Austen

LEFT The Rice portrait of Jane Austen that has been the subject of debate and controversy

CLASSIC LITERATURE

RIGHT The Royal Crescent in Bath, the height of fashion in Regency times

embarrassment, Jane was adamant in her decision and returned as quickly as possible to her family in Bath.

When George Austen died in 1805, the family's income was considerably reduced and Cassandra and her daughters – who were the only two remaining "children" at home – had to rely on support from the girls' brothers and the small sum of money left to young Cassandra by her fiancé, Thomas Fowle (who had died of yellow fever in the Caribbean in 1797). Fowle had travelled overseas to take up a post as military chaplain. He and Cassandra had been engaged for many years prior to his death and had been unable to marry due to a lack of money. Reverend Austen would not have had a great deal financially to give either of his daughters for marriage. After a brief stay in Clifton in 1806, that same year, mother and daughters moved to Southampton where Jane wrote about her "happy escape" from Bath. Being in Southampton the family were now close to the two youngest sons, Frank and Charles, who were still based in Portsmouth. They lived with Frank and his family. Then, in 1809, the family moved once again. This time, the move took them to Chawton, near Winchester, where the now wealthy Edward provided a cottage for his mother and sisters on one of his estates.

Having sold *Northanger Abbey* to a publisher before leaving Southampton, Jane resumed her quest for a publisher and revised *Sense And Sensibility* which was accepted for publication around late 1810 or early 1811. It was published anonymously in 1811 – the author writes under the pen name of "A Lady" – which received fairly favourable reviews and eventually the first edition gave Jane a profit of £140. Encouraged by the novel's success, she went on to revise *Pride And Prejudice* and sold the manuscript in 1812 for a flat fee of £110. Publication took place in January 1813 while *Mansfield Park* was firmly underway. The third novel was published in May 1814 following the second edition of *Sense And Sensibility* which appeared in October 1813. The author was already hard at work on *Emma*

CLASSIC LITERATURE

ABOVE Chawton
where her principal
novels were written

which was published in December 1815 and dedicated to the Prince Regent. The
following year, a second edition of *Mansfield Park* was published but failed to reach
the same sales potential as the 1814 first edition. For 12 months from August 1815,
Jane would work steadily on *Persuasion* and it was during this time that Jane began
to suffer from illness.

The author was particularly influenced by the likes of Henry Fielding (1707–1754) the English novelist and dramatist renowned for his earthy humour and satirical prowess. As well as writing the famous novel *Tom Jones*, the aristocratic Fielding was also the founder of the Bow Street Runners – the forerunner to London's "Bobbies" and ultimate police force. Unlike Fielding who gave his characters little emotional depth, although he was the first author to openly admit that his prose fiction was pure artefact, Austen gave her characters immense depth.

She was also influenced by Fielding's rival and peer, Samuel Richardson (1689-1761) who is perhaps best known for his novels *Pamela: Or, Virtue Rewarded* (1740), *Clarissa: Or, The History Of A Young Lady* (1748) and *Sir Charles Grandison* (1753). However, Richardson's writing was typical of his time and he chose to "hide" the fictional nature of his works by using the guise of "letters" written by the protagonist to give his prose more recognition and clout with the 18th century readership. But, like Fielding and Jane Austen later on, he was keen to explore the moralistic values of his time and *Pamela* became a publishing sensation.

Another influence on Austen was her peer Sir Walter Scott (1771-1832), the Scottish historical novelist and poet who enjoyed a prolific career on an international level with readerships in Europe, Australia and North America during his lifetime. Among his most famous works are *Ivanhoe, Rob Roy, The Lady Of The Lake* and *Waverley*. Jane was also influenced by Samuel Johnson, William Cowper, Fanny Burney and George Crabbe.

She was widely, if moderately revered during her lifetime and some critics thought her novels too repetitive and overtly "moral". But the plots were well constructed and she received particular praise from Sir Walter Scott who deemed Austen's attention to detail and the depiction of the ordinary feelings of her characters as exquisite. Another fan was the Prince Regent who instructed his librarian to give Jane a guided tour of his London library. Macaulay, Taylor Coleridge, Southey and FitzGerald were also ardent admirers of her work. However, there was one famous literary giant that Jane Austen failed to impress: the American, Mark Twain, who said: "Jane Austen? Why, I go so far as to say that any library is a good library that does not contain a volume by Jane Austen. Even if it contains no other book." Despite the fact that Anne Brontë was often regarded as a writer with "Jane Austen qualities", her sister, Charlotte Brontë, was also indifferent to her fellow writer and criticised the narrow scope of Austen's fiction. However, other writers, including Rudyard Kipling, were huge Austen admirers. Kipling even wrote *The Janeites,* a short story about a group of soldiers who were ardent Jane Austen fans.

Jane began work on *Sanditon* in early 1817 but gave up on the novel in March. April that same year saw the 41-year-old author write her will where she left most of what she had to her sister, Cassandra. Jane Austen was moved to Winchester, to rented rooms, by Cassandra for medical treatment for suspected Addison's disease which occurs when the adrenal glands do not produce enough of the hormone cortisol (and, in some cases, the hormone aldosterone). Sometimes known as adrenal insufficiency, the disease can cause weight loss, muscle weakness, fatigue, low blood

LEFT Richardson realism impressed by the young Jane

RIGHT Winchester Cathedral where Jane Austen was buried

pressure and sometimes darkening of the skin. The disease was particularly common (however unnamed) during the 19th century as a further complication of tuberculosis. In Jane's case it proved fatal and the author died in her sister's arms on Friday 18 July 1817.

She was buried at Winchester Cathedral on 24 July in the north aisle with the interesting inscription on her grave that mentions the author's "sweetness of her temper" and references her Christian humility. However, it is clear from both Jane Austen's novels and her letters – particularly to Cassandra – that she was far more than a "sweet" ordinary woman. The inscription also doesn't mention the author's literary prowess, but this is perhaps not surprising, considering that all her works were published anonymously and each advertised "Written by A Lady", something that was not uncommon at the time. Her family mourned her deeply and their feelings were summed up in the words of the poem by James Austen:

In her, rare union, were combined a fair form,
And a fairer mind;
Hers fancy quick, and clear good sense,
And wit which never gave offence;
A heart as warm as ever beat,
A temper even; calm and sweet.

Though quick and keen her mental eye
Poor nature's foibles to espy,
And seemed forever on the watch,
Some trails of ridicule to catch
Yet not a word she ever penned
Which hurt the feelings of a friend.

Chapter 1

Austen Country

Nestling in a quiet spot between Basingstoke and Winchester lies the village of Steventon, birthplace and home to Jane for more than half her life. As a keen walker, Austen would often walk to Popham Lane where she would collect the family post from a building known today as the Wheatsheaf Inn. The family home, the rectory in Steventon, had seven bedrooms and the 17th century house was repaired during the 1760s for the arrival of Reverend Austen and his family. The Reverend was known to farm the fields surrounding his home, while his wife grew potatoes (quite an innovation at the time) and formal gardens with a turf walkway and a grassy bank marked the grounds. The driveway was built to receive carriages and a barn – situated in the grounds – where the family performed their elaborate plays and comic theatricals for friends and family. However, during winter months, all performances were given in the more formal surroundings of the dining room. A private footpath of hedgerows and mixed shrubs was later cultivated to provide a pathway for the family to the church while chestnut trees, firs and elms adorned one side of the rectory. Sadly, today, the rectory is gone.

Much of the dilapidated property was demolished soon after the author's death, however, the 12th century church, where Jane worshipped with her family, is virtually unchanged and remains very much as it would have done during her father's time and later when her oldest brother, James, took over the parish (from

LEFT Despite its
beauty, Jane never
commented on Bath's
architecture

CLASSIC LITERATURE

RIGHT The Circus in
Bath

CLASSIC LITERATURE

his father). The church now houses a bronze plaque dedicated to the author while her brother is buried in the churchyard.

When James Austen died, Henry became the rector at Steventon until he was replaced by William Knight (Edward's son) in 1822. Following his retirement from the military and then the banking world (after he faced bankruptcy) Henry Austen became a member of the clergy in 1816 and became perpetual curate at Bentley, near Alton, where he stayed until 1839. As well as attending dances and social evenings at the Assembly Rooms in Basingstoke, Jane and Cassandra were also invited to a number of dances held in nearby large houses. The Vyne, now a National Trust property, on the outskirts of Basingstoke is one such venue, while Ibthorpe was home to the Lloyd family (Mary Lloyd later became James Austen's second wife). After being tenants of the Austens, the Lloyd family moved to Ibthorpe in 1792. When Mrs Lloyd died in 1805 (the same year as Reverend George Austen), Martha Lloyd, Mary's sister, moved to Bath to live with Cassandra and her two daughters and later travelled with the family to Southampton and eventually Chawton. Martha remained with the family for around 20 years.

When Jane's parents moved to Bath on her father's retirement in 1801, she was not best pleased at having to move from her childhood home in the country. There has been much speculation that Jane detested Bath, however some writers who have observed her life and works disagree and offer the suggestion that her first impressions were tempered by her dismay at leaving her country home. There is some evidence in chronicles of her everyday life that even though the young author grew more accustomed to the crowds (and pavements) she still sometimes took refuge in the Gardens and any other place that offered her natural beauty and charm. She was clearly bothered that Bath was, in fact, not Steventon.

Bath was particularly preoccupied with material wealth at the beginning of the 19th century and Jane was forced to tolerate it. However, what is clear in Austen's

novels is that Bath gave the writer an extended experience of the contemporary society that she wished to write about. What Jane did love about Bath, despite the fact she disliked its urban lifestyle, was its openness to a myriad of ideas, sights, sounds and interpretations. Interestingly, Jane never commented on the wonder of Bath's architecture, either in her letters or novels, however the city was in its heyday

CLASSIC LITERATURE

and its golden stone buildings were immaculate. She didn't even mention the famous Roman Baths, the Circus, the most beautiful piece of civil design in the country, or the outstanding Royal Crescent. To Jane Austen, a building was an indication of wealth, rather than taste and all biographies about the author imply that Bath crushed her writing style and greatly discouraged her.

However, Nigel Nicholson, writing in *The Spectator,* December 2003, believes that these notions are misguided. He writes that Jane was already discouraged by the time she arrived in Bath and that the rejection of *Pride And Prejudice* had greatly contributed to her lack of writing before the move – and she had attempted nothing new for two years. He also states that Jane's letters to Cassandra prove she was becoming reconciled to the move and that she was ready for a change of scene. She was bored with the social circles in Basingstoke and with her brothers having moved away from home to follow their respective careers there was nothing much left for the remainder of the family in Steventon. As a united family, Nicholson also suggests, that while living at 4 Sydney Place, opposite Sydney Gardens, the Austens had a far wider interest in politics, religion, literature and the war than Jane's letters and novels suggest. He argues that the family enjoyed their life in Bath in their Georgian home. He also suggests that with Jane's keenness for new experiences and "playful disposition" that it is "difficult to imagine her moping at home."

After five years, and the death of her father, Jane, her mother, sister and Martha Lloyd were set to move again. The move, this time, took them to Southampton to the rented lodgings of Naval Captain Frank Austen and his family. Frank and Mary Austen's first child (they would have 11 in total) was on the way and the lodgings proved expensive for the family, so they all moved to an old fashioned house in Castle Square which was rented from the Marquess of Lansdowne. The garden ran along the old city walls of Southampton which overlooked the river and the family had access to the promenade which ran the length of the walls.

LEFT The Pump Room was part of the social heart of Bath in Austen's day

CLASSIC LITERATURE

During the early 19th century, Southampton was still a medieval town and the house would have looked westwards across the beautiful Southampton Water. Family excursions included river trips on the River Itchen to Netley Abbey and Jane still had a love of walking and she was known to have walked along the banks of the Itchen and the Test rivers as well as Southampton Water and the surrounding countryside. She and Cassandra continued to attend dances, some of which were held at the Dolphin Hotel (still in existence today), but financial constraints tapered their socialising to some degree. Visits to the New Forest were a firm favourite with the Austen family who enjoyed seeing the outstanding scenery and famous wild ponies. They travelled the Beaulieu River and visited Beaulieu Abbey and the famous shipbuilding yards at Bucklers Hard.

Cassandra Austen had only intended the move to Southampton as temporary and after three years she moved her two daughters and their house guest, Martha Lloyd, to Chawton cottage in Chawton, near Alton where they set up home in the former bailiff's house on the Chawton estate. It was here that Jane would find her true "literary home" where she wrote on a small round table in the parlour. Her life was somewhat quieter at Chawton and she resumed her career in a home surrounded by old varieties of flowers and herbs in a pretty garden. Despite taking up writing again, each day Jane and Cassandra would walk and they also went shopping in nearby Alton. The area was steeped in history with the village's earliest records appearing in the Domesday survey of 1086. The present Chawton House was built during the time of the Armada (1588) and was eventually passed down to Elizabeth Knight (who had two husbands who were both required to change their surname to Knight). Today, the "Jane Austen's House Museum", as Chawton cottage is known, is open to the public and receives 30,000 visitors a year.

LEFT Jane Austen's house is now a museum

BELOW The Winchester house in which Jane Austen lived her final days

She also regularly visited her niece, Anna Lefroy, the oldest daughter of her brother James and his first wife, Ann Mathew. It is Anna's memoirs about both her aunts, Cassandra and Jane, that provides a great deal of information about one of the world's most celebrated writers. The bodies of both Cassandra Austen, and her daughter, Cassandra, are buried at St Nicholas's Church, a short distance from Chawton. The church itself was destroyed by fire sometime later and was rebuilt in 1872.

Chawton House was restored to establish a Centre of the Study of Early English Women's Writing 1600-1830, and now houses more than 9,000 volumes and related manuscripts in the renowned Chawton House Library.

CLASSIC LITERATURE

Chapter 2

The Novels

Jane Austen is particularly noted for her meticulous attention to detail and witty observations about early 19th century English society. Combining romantic comedy with social satire and psychological insight, Jane confidently portrays the quiet, day-to-day lives of members of the upper middle classes. Her novels generally consist of two themes: loss of illusion (which challenges her main characters to adopt a more mature outlook) and the struggle between traditional moral ideals and how to reconcile these with the demands of everyday life. Many of the novels weave a pattern of characters learning by their mistakes, with Jane Austen's insight into human nature showing her exceptional skill for a well thought out psychological approach and discussion. It was these strengths that led to the author becoming classed as one of the greatest novelists (and creator of the modern-day novel) of the 19th and 20th centuries.

CLASSIC LITERATURE

LEFT Elinor Dashwood talking to Lucy Steele in a scene from Jane Austen's *Sense And Sensibility*

FAR LEFT
A hand written letter by Jane Austen

CLASSIC LITERATURE

Sense And Sensibility (1811)

Although not Austen's first novel, *Sense And Sensibility* was her first published work. Originally entitled *Elinor And Marianne*, the book was revisited by Jane and submitted to Thomas Egerton in London for publication under its new name, with the first edition appearing in 1811. The plot centres around two sisters, as its original title would suggest, 19-year-old Elinor – the heroine – (known for her sense) and 17-year-old Marianne (renowned for her sensibility, ie, emotion).

When the sisters' father, Henry Dashwood, dies leaving the family home at Norland and all his money to his first wife's son, John, his second wife and three daughters, Elinor, Marianne and 13-year-old Margaret are left with no permanent home and little income. Their plight is largely brought about by John's wife, Fanny Dashwood (and sister to Edward and Robert Ferrars) who with her manipulative and scheming ways persuades her husband to leave the four women virtually penniless. For his part, John Dashwood seems unconcerned with the situation he leaves his stepmother and three half-sisters in. As a result, they are invited to stay with distant relatives, the Middletons, at Barton Park in Barton Cottage. For Elinor, the move is a sad one, due to her recent blossoming relationship with Edward Ferrars, the brother-in-law of John Dashwood. But life at Barton Park provides the sisters with new experiences and many new acquaintances, including retired officer and confirmed bachelor, Colonel Bandon and the impetuous John Willoughby. When Marianne twists her ankle running down a hill, she is rescued by the gallant Willoughby in the rain and from then on he openly courts Marianne. The two are unabashed in their affections and deliberately flaunt their attachment. Willoughby leaves a miserable and lovesick Marianne at Barton Park when he suddenly announces that he must leave at once for business in London.

CLASSIC LITERATURE

RIGHT Illustration by
Hugh Thomson from
Sense and Sensibility

Two recently discovered relatives of Lady Middleton's mother, Mrs Jennings,
arrive at Barton Park as additional house guests. Anne and Lucy Steele do not bring
good fortune for Elinor as Lucy admits to her that she has secretly been engaged to
Mr Ferrars for one year. Initially Elinor assumes Lucy means Edward's younger
brother, Robert, but is extremely shocked and heartbroken to learn that she means
her own love, Edward.

Mrs Jennings invites Elinor and Marianne to London to stay with her, where the
older sister learns from Colonel Brandon that there is news of the engagement
between Willoughby and Marianne. However, this is a new revelation to her
family. Meanwhile the well-intentioned Mrs Jennings is trying to marry off the two

sisters as quickly as possible. Marianne is particularly excited to meet with Willoughby at a party in town but he cruelly rejects his once love. She is further hurt by a letter she receives not long after in which her former love denies that he ever had any feelings for her. Some insight is given to Elinor by Colonel Brandon who confirms that Willoughby has, in the past, treated other young women the same way and possesses a callousness that is then confirmed by Mrs Jennings who also informs them that having squandered his fortune, the debauched young man has become engaged to the wealthy heiress, Miss Sophia Grey.

When Anne Steele lets slip that her younger sister is secretly engaged to Edward Ferrars, his mother is outraged and promptly disinherits him, and the family fortune is promised to Robert. Meanwhile, Elinor and Marianne visit friends (the Palmer family) in Cleveland on their return trip from London. Here, Marianne develops a severe cold – having taken many long walks in the rain – and she becomes gravely ill. On hearing of Marianne's plight, Willoughby decides to visit seeking forgiveness for his uncaring behaviour and offering an explanation for his ill-mannered treatment of her. Elinor takes pity on the hapless young man and shares his story with her sister. However, Marianne realises that she would never have been happy with Willoughby while she slowly returns to health. Her mother and Colonel Brandon arrive at Cleveland and are relieved to find a convalescing Marianne. The family eventually return to Barton Park where they learn the news that Lucy Steele and Mr Ferrars are engaged and wrongly assume that the groom-to-be is indeed Edward. However, his arrival at Barton Park serves to confirm that actually, money-grabbing Lucy Steele is in fact engaged to Robert Ferrars now that he will inherit from his mother. It allows Edward the chance to finally propose to Elinor while Colonel Brandon seeks Marianne's hand in marriage. The retired officer fell in love with Marianne early in the story and was always kind, honourable and gracious in his dealings with the family. While Mrs Dashwood and Margaret remain at Barton

CLASSIC LITERATURE

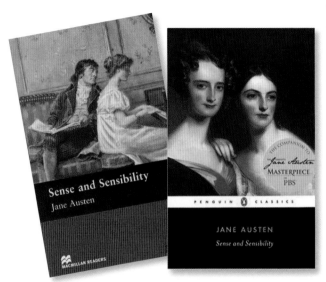

ABOVE & RIGHT
Sense and Sensiblity has
been published many
times over the years and
is an international
favourite

Park, the two couples live together, close by at Delaford.

Sense and sensibility are commonly analysed by the author throughout and the distinction between the two is clearly symbolised by the characters of Elinor and Marianne Dashwood. Elinor demonstrates reason, restraint, social responsibility and all the qualities that adhere to "sense" with her clear headed concern for the welfare of others. In contrast, Marianne represents emotion, spontaneity, devotion and impulsiveness which is evident in her relationship with John Willoughby which she openly and unashamedly flaunts; Elinor, however, is more discreet about her feelings for Edward Ferrars. They represent completely differing temperaments throughout the novel in their attitudes to love and how they express their feelings.

As an author, Jane Austen did not fit neatly into any particular writing era. She was too early to be Victorian and a little too late to belong to the Regency era, and this shows in the cultural and historical resonances through the dichotomy between "sense" and "sensibility" and the fact that Austen was writing in the middle of two cultural movements: Classicism and Romanticism. Elinor Dashwood represents the 18th century neo-classicism and the author is using this character to allude to propriety, economic practicalities and perspective. However, the novel was just beginning to develop as a literary genre and Marianne leads towards the "cult of sensibility" that was threatening to emerge representing romance, imagination, idealism and excess. The novel definitely reminds the reader that the literary landscape was changing at that time. Austen was keen to emphasise that a woman's social standing was improved (quite literally) by marriage and her novels ultimately lead to the marriage of the heroine. The Dashwood sisters were no exception.

But *Sense And Sensibility* wasn't that straightforward. Indeed, Elinor did not lack passion, and Marianne, was not always foolish and headstrong. What Austen actually did with the characters was to use their fundamental characteristics as a starting point for dialogue. The

happiness that the formerly impoverished sisters find, towards the end of the novel, comes about as a result of their willingness to learn from each other and their life experiences. Austen, perhaps, was trying to teach and encourage everyday people, through her wit and observations, that this was what life was actually about. Neither sense nor sensibility prevails; the author provides a logical balance between the two. This led to some criticism that the ending was a disappointment, especially as Marianne marries a man whom she had not thought she could love. But the comic and subtle ironies used to describe characters such as the Middletons, Lucy Steele and Mrs Jennings helped to persuade readers, both past and present, that *Sense And Sensibility* is Austen at her best.

CLASSIC LITERATURE

Pride And Prejudice (1813)

Publishing *Pride And Prejudice* under the pen name of "A Lady" may not have given Jane Austen the recognition she deserved for her work, however it did serve to provide her with anonymity at a time when English society associated a woman's presence in public life as a form of degradation in an atmosphere of repression. She was a realist, who poked fun at the snobbishness of the gentry and sometimes the poor breeding of those lower down the social scale, however, Austen depicted social advancement throughout her novels and the appropriate behaviour for each gender in an expert manner. Young men, for example, were advanced by their entry to the military or the church or through birth, while young women would find a firm social footing if they acquired wealth, i.e. marriage. This novel was no exception. In fact, the opening sentence sums up the subject matter right from the start, "It is a truth universally acknowledged, that a man in possession of a good fortune must be in want of a wife."

The young and extremely wealthy Charles Bingley rents Netherfield Park, a manor house, at the start of the novel, which causes a stir in the neighbouring village of Longbourn. It causes a particular sensation in the household where five unmarried daughters, Jane, Elizabeth, Mary, Kitty and Lydia are all desperately seeking a future husband. However, Mr, with his modest income, does not have a great deal of wealth to share between five daughters and their potential nuptials. The nosey and irrepressible Mrs has but one goal in life: to marry off her daughters. But her poor background and sometimes less than acceptable social behaviour often puts off any potential suitors for her daughters. Mr pays a social visit to Mr Bingley and

CLASSIC LITERATURE

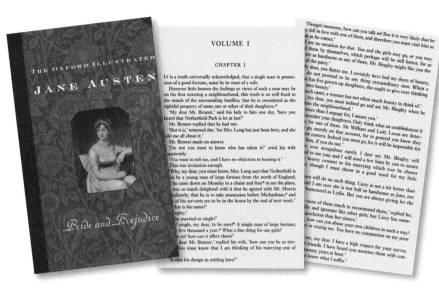

VOLUME I

CHAPTER I

It is a truth universally acknowledged, that a single man in possession of a good fortune, must be in want of a wife.

However little known the feelings or views of such a man may be
on his first entering a neighbourhood, this truth is so well fixed in
the minds of the surrounding families, that he is considered as the
rightful property of some one or other of their daughters.*

'My dear Mr. Bennet,' said his lady to him one day, 'have you
heard that Netherfield Park is let at last?'

Mr. Bennet replied that he had not.

'But it is,' returned she; 'for Mrs. Long has just been here, and she
told me all about it.'

Mr. Bennet made no answer.

'Do not you want to know who has taken it?' cried his wife
impatiently.

'You want to tell me, and I have no objection to hearing it.'

This was invitation enough.

'Why, my dear, you must know, Mrs. Long says that Netherfield is
taken by a young man of large fortune from the north of England;
that he came down on Monday in a chaise and four* to see the place,
and was so much delighted with it that he agreed with Mr. Morris
immediately; that he is to take possession before Michaelmas,* and
some of his servants are to be in the house by the end of next week.'

'What is his name?'

'Bingley.'

'Is he married or single?'

'Oh! single, my dear, to be sure!* A single man of large fortune;
four or five thousand a year.* What a fine thing for our girls!'

'How so? how can it affect them?'

'My dear Mr. Bennet,' replied his wife, 'how can you be so tire-
some! You must know that I am thinking of his marrying one of
them.'

'Is that his design in settling here?'

'Design! nonsense, how can you talk so! But it is very likely that he
may fall in love with one of them, and therefore you must visit him as
soon as he comes.'

'I see no occasion for that. You and the girls may go, or you may
send them by themselves, which perhaps will be still better, for as
you are as handsome as any of them, Mr. Bingley might like you the
best of the party.'

'My dear, you flatter me. I certainly have had my share of beauty,
but I do not pretend to be any thing extraordinary now. When a
woman has five grown up daughters, she ought to give over thinking
of her own beauty.'

'In such cases, a woman has not often much beauty to think of.'

'But, my dear, you must indeed go and see Mr. Bingley when he
comes into the neighbourhood.'

'It is more than I engage for, I assure you.'

'But consider your daughters. Only think what an establishment it
would be for one of them. Sir William and Lady Lucas are deter-
mined to go, merely on that account, for in general you know they
do not visit new comers. Indeed you must go, for it will be impossible for
us to visit him, if you do not.'

'You are over scrupulous surely. I dare say Mr. Bingley will
be very glad to see you; and I will send a few lines by you to assure
him of my hearty consent to his marrying which ever he chuses
of the girls; though I must throw in a good word for my little
Lizzy.'

'I desire you will do no such thing. Lizzy is not a bit better than
the others; and I am sure she is not half so handsome as Jane, nor
half so good humoured as Lydia. But you are always giving her the
preference.'

'They have none of them much to recommend them,' replied he;
'they are all silly and ignorant like other girls; but Lizzy has something more of quickness than her sisters.'

'Mr. Bennet, how can you abuse your own children in such a way?
You take delight in vexing me. You have no compassion on my poor
nerves.'

'You mistake me, my dear. I have a high respect for your nerves.
They are my old friends. I have heard you mention them with con-
sideration these twenty years at least.'

'Ah! you do not know what I suffer.'

the family are invited to attend a ball at which Charles will be present.

Charles is immediately taken with Jane and spends much of the evening dancing
with her while his close friend – Fitzwilliam Darcy – is disenchanted with
proceedings and flatly refuses to dance with Elizabeth (Mr's most loved daughter)
whom he describes as uninteresting. His stubbornness to accept those with less social
standing than himself causes the guests at the ball to view Darcy as arrogant and
obnoxious. Over the course of the social calendar, however, he finds himself drawn
to Elizabeth's intelligence and charm. Jane and Charles's relationship continues to
blossom and she decides to visit him at home. Caught in a torrential downpour on
the way to Netherfield Park, Jane becomes ill and she is forced to remain at the

manor house for several days. Elizabeth finds herself wading through muddy fields to take care of her older sister and arrives bedraggled and mud spattered, much to the disdain of Charles's sister, the snobbish Miss Bingley. She is further spited when she discovers that Darcy, whom she herself has her eye on, is quite taken with Elizabeth.

When Jane is well enough to return home, she, and Elizabeth find Mr Collins, a pompous and snobbish clergyman visiting their father. He is the heir to the family home (as an entailed property the house can only be passed to male relatives) and he quickly makes a proposal of marriage to Elizabeth. His pride is severely wounded when he is rejected but meanwhile, the sisters have made acquaintances with military officers based in a nearby town. One particular officer, George Wickham strikes up a friendship with Elizabeth and he explains to her that Darcy once cruelly cheated him out of his inheritance. During the winter, Jane is dismayed to learn that Charles, his sister and Darcy have returned to London. Mr Collins becomes engaged to Charlotte Lucas (Elizabeth's closest friend) and the family are shocked that the daughter of a local knight is marrying for financial security. The marriage, however, goes ahead and Elizabeth promises to visit her friend in her new home.

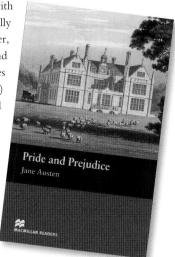

Pride and Prejudice
Jane Austen

MACMILLAN READERS

Jane makes the journey to London to visit friends of her own and is disappointed when Charles makes no effort to visit her. She does, however, receive his sister who is less than gracious. It seems as if Mrs's endeavours to find her daughter's suitable matches may well have been in vain. Unbeknown

CLASSIC LITERATURE

to the Bennets, however, Darcy is more and more taken with Elizabeth while Miss Bingley tries extremely hard to gain his attention. The fact that Elizabeth is not openly pursuing him, in the same way her rival is, makes her all the more endearing. In the spring, Elizabeth keeps her promise to Charlotte and visits her friend who lives close by to Lady Catherine de Bourgh, who happens to be Mr Collins's patron, as well as Darcy's aunt. Here the two meet again and from then on, Darcy begins to visit Mr Collins and Charlotte fairly regularly. But, his unexpected and shocking marriage proposal is quickly rejected by Elizabeth and she tells her suitor he is rude, unpleasant and that she does not agree with his manipulation of keeping Charles Bingley away from Jane. She also scolds him for cheating Wickham out of his inheritance. Following their disagreement Darcy writes to Elizabeth and explains that he did indeed advise Bingley to distance himself from Jane, but not because the couple might not be suited; he claims that he thought the relationship might not be serious enough. He also explains that Wickham is a liar and that the real reason they fell out was because the young officer had attempted to elope with Darcy's shy younger sister, Georgiana. Elizabeth finds herself re-evaluating her feelings for the man she once thought arrogant and obnoxious and on her return home is cold towards her former friend, George Wickham. The younger Bennet sisters are rather heartbroken when the military officers are to be stationed elsewhere and Lydia persuades her father to let her spend the summer in Brighton – home of their new barracks – with an old colonel and friend of the family. In June, Elizabeth travels north with the Gardiner family (distant relatives) where she arrives in Pemberley near to where Darcy has an estate. Having made sure that Darcy is not at home, Elizabeth visits the estate and finds she is very taken with the marvellous house and grounds. She also hears from Darcy's servants that he is a kind and generous master. Darcy makes a sudden appearance and invites Elizabeth and the Gardiners to stay. He also wishes to introduce Elizabeth to his sister, Georgiana.

Lydia and Wickham, meanwhile, elope and the news from home suggests that the young couple are living out of wedlock. Worried by the disgrace it would surely bring on her family, Elizabeth hurries home and her father, aided by Mr Gardiner set out to find Lydia. The search proves futile and the family face despair. However, Mr Gardiner eventually finds the couple and writes to the Bennet household to say

LEFT Groombridge Place, Longbourn, the Bennet family home

CLASSIC LITERATURE

that Wickham has agreed to marry Lydia in return for an annual income. The entire family are convinced that Gardiner has paid Wickham off, but it comes to light that it is in fact Darcy that is maintaining the officer and his wife. Darcy has brought the Bennet family salvation. The newlyweds arrive in Longbourn and stay briefly. Mr Bennet is cold towards his daughter and son-in-law before they depart for Wickham's new assignment in the north of England. Meanwhile, Charles Bingley returns to his rented manor house and resumes his courtship of Jane Bennet. Darcy returns also and often visits the Bennets but makes no reference to his earlier proposal or his earlier desire to marry Elizabeth. Everyone is delighted when Charles proposes to Jane, however. All, that is, except his calculating, cold sister, Miss Bingley. Lady Catherine then decides to visit Longbourn where she takes Elizabeth to one side and tells the young woman of Darcy's intention to marry her. But Lady Catherine considers them an unsuitable match and insists that Elizabeth refuse her nephew's proposal. Elizabeth confirms she is not engaged to Darcy, but she refuses to answer anything that will affect her own happiness. While out walking with Darcy she accepts his second proposal. As is customary, Austen's heroines are married and find their much sought-after, social standing.

This much-cherished love story is as popular today as it was in Austen's own time. And, as with all good stories, took the couple in question through a labyrinth of trials and tribulations before their love could be united and result in ultimate happiness. Initially, Elizabeth judges Darcy on her first impression through pride, while Darcy, for his part, judges Elizabeth through his own prejudice of her poorer social standing. With interference from Lady Catherine, snobbery from Miss Bingley and idiocy from Mrs Bennet, it seems as if true love will be lost in the anxieties of social connections, however, the truth overcomes these obstacles and conquers in the end. But, ever the realist, Austen also uses the character of Charlotte (and her marriage to Mr Collins) to portray that sometimes the head rather than the

heart dictates fate and that sometimes it is money and financial security that may be the conqueror. The novel depicts just how important it is for a woman to ensure her reputation and that women are expected to behave in certain ways. Reputation is shown as of vital importance when Lydia elopes with Wickham and lives out of wedlock. One of the main symbols or motifs of the novel is the sense of journeys. Each journey undertaken by the characters, however short, functions as a catalyst for change. Perhaps Austen was seeking changes in social structures and their interference in everyday lives, or perhaps she was merely accepting of the inevitable lack of change that society alluded to at that time.

CLASSIC LITERATURE

Mansfield Park (1814)

Appearing in print in 1814, *Mansfield Park* was written between 1811 and 1813. As is usual in a novel by Austen, this proves to be no exception to the rule with regard to social standing, however, it goes further than any of the other titles in its social awareness. Here, Jane focuses on the slave trade and the roots of the British aristocracy's corruption and exploitation of others which helps to classify *Mansfield Park* as one of the author's least romantic works.

Young Fanny Price is sent to live with her wealthy relatives, Sir Thomas and Lady Bertram. Her mother, unlike her sister, Lady Bertram, married beneath her and Fanny's family are fairly poor and live in fairly squalid surroundings. Her father, a disabled sailor, drinks heavily, but life is not a bed of roses for Fanny at Mansfield Park either where she is consistently abused by another of her aunts, Mrs Norris, who runs the Bertrams' estate. Fanny finds a friend in Edmund Bertram, who is planning to join the clergy while his older brother, Tom, is a drunk and his sisters, Maria and Julia, more intent on marrying well and continuing their fashionable status than anything else. Fanny lives in a repressive environment and becomes shy and deferential. While Sir Thomas is away in Antigua attending to his plantations, Henry and Mary Crawford (the brother and sister of the local minister's wife) arrive and with their cheerful and witty dispositions soon become an integral part of the Mansfield set. Henry flirts openly with Maria who by now is engaged to the wealthy, but boring, Rushworth, who provides comic relief throughout the novel with his idiotic comments. When it suits him, Henry is also prone to flirting with Julia, however, his sister, Mary is initially only interested in Tom. However, she begins to find him boring and uninterested in her so she finds herself increasingly attracted to Edmund. But she doesn't want to marry a clergyman and Fanny (although she doesn't want to admit it to herself) has quietly fallen in love with the younger brother.

Tom's friend, Yates, soon comes to visit and suggests that the party put on a play. The idea is eagerly received by everyone except Edmund and Fanny, who are both horrified by the suggestion that they should act. The play goes ahead despite their protestations (Edmund even has to play a part) and there are some racy scenes acted out. Fanny is pressured to step in at the last moment and is virtually forced to concede against her wishes, however, Sir Thomas arrives home suddenly from his plantations. He is not best pleased with the play and quickly puts a stop to the nonsense as he calls it. Maria is married to Rushworth – when Henry fails to declare his love – and she and Julia set out for London. Edmund, meanwhile almost proposes to Mary on a number of occasions, but her cynical thoughts over his becoming a member of the

ABOVE Billie Piper had a starring role in the television adaption of *Mansfield Park*

clergy change his mind at the last moment. Edmund confides in Fanny who is upset by his revelations, however, she is being wooed by Henry (as a laugh) who surprises himself by finding he is actually in love with her. Meanwhile, Fanny has become indispensable as far as her uncle and aunt are concerned and when William, her brother, arrives they give a ball in her honour. Henry then helps William gain promotion in the navy and using this as leverage proposes to Fanny who refuses him. Sir Thomas is upset by his niece's refusal of a wealthy man and as a punishment Fanny is sent home.

CLASSIC LITERATURE

Edmund is ordained and continues to debate his feelings for Mary, much to Fanny's dismay. Henry refuses to give up on Fanny and while he's away on business, Mary writes to her to encourage her to accept her brother's proposal. Fate takes a hand when a series of unexpected events happen in rapid

ABOVE & RIGHT
Mansfield Park television adaptation, 2007

succession. Tom falls dangerously ill (a result of his constant partying) and Henry's business trip turns out to be his excuse so he can escape and elope with the married Maria. Julia, in a knee-jerk reaction, elopes with Yates and Fanny is requested back at Mansfield. She arrives with her younger sister, Susan, and finds that Edmund has finally seen through Mary. She had openly wished Tom's illness would kill him so that Edmund would inherit. At this news Edmund turns to Fanny for consolation. While Henry and Maria's relationship doesn't last – she moves to the Continent with Mrs Norris – Julia and Yates are eventually reconciled to the family and Edmund finally marries Fanny. Susan takes up her sister's role within the Bertram household and all is well again.

The novel is extremely complicated even though the crux is the lead character's quest to find social status, which she does eventually through marriage to Edmund. With no way in which to have a professional life, Fanny's only option is to marry for security and status. The novel heralds virtue and those characters who show promise are destined for an agreeable fate, while those who act inappropriately or selfishly are not. What is clear is that Austen is questioning whether people can change. Certainly, Sir Thomas and Edmund seem to have learned from their experiences, however, Maria, Mary and Henry don't appear to have learnt anything. Using both the City and country life as a backdrop to events, Jane appears to be implying that the town provides a life of vice while the country teaches all that is good. However, she complicates things by portraying country characters with faults and town characters with healthy reputations and her sexual awareness is particularly acute in this book, despite the fact that it would probably have been rather too direct in its approach during the early 19th century. Perhaps it is this that led to *Mansfield Park* becoming one of Austen's most controversial novels and least popular of her works. However, there is a great deal of satire in the novel and it is probably the most socially realistic.

CLASSIC LITERATURE

Emma (1815)

Austen began writing Emma in January 1814 and finished the novel just over a year later in March 1815. Published in three volumes, it was the fourth and last novel that Jane would see in print during her lifetime. An initial print-run saw 2,000 copies ready for sale, but more than a quarter remained unsold at the end of the following four years. The profits for Austen were paltry. She earned less than £40 from the book before her death a year and a half after publication.

Written in a comic tone, the novel tells the story of Emma Woodhouse, who like all other Austen heroines finds her destiny in marriage. However, at the start of the story, Emma is convinced that despite being, in her own view, a natural at making good love matches, she will never marry.

Having gained a modicum of success in bringing her governess, Miss Taylor, together with Mr Weston, a widower, Emma decides to act as matchmaker for her newly acquired friend, Harriet Smith. Despite the fact that Harriet's parentage is unknown, Emma decides that she should ultimately be a gentleman's wife and sets about trying to pair her to the village rector, Mr Elton. However, Harriet is taken with Robert Martin, a wealthy farmer, and Emma advises her friend to reject his proposal.

Harriet quickly becomes infatuated with Elton, however, he is more interested in Emma and her matchmaking plans go awry. Emma has one critic, her friend and brother-in-law, Mr George Knightley who watches her matchmaking efforts with some cynicism and firmly believes that Harriet and Robert Martin would be well suited to one another. With Harriet's lack of knowledge about her past, he also believes that Harriet would be lucky to marry Martin. Meanwhile, Elton who

ABOVE Emma, novel

RIGHT A scene from Jane Austen's novel *Emma*

CLASSIC LITERATURE

has been rejected by Emma and offended at the suggestion that Harriet could possibly be his equal, leaves the village of Highbury and arrives in Bath where he marries a young woman almost immediately.

Comforting an upset Harriet, who has become somewhat a victim of her friend's meddling, Emma is left pondering who Frank Churchill is. Churchill is, in fact, the son of Mr Weston and was brought up by his aunt and uncle in London when his mother died. He has obviously come to visit his father and his new wife in Highbury and would have come sooner had it not been for his aunt's many illnesses and complaints. Knightley is immediately suspicious of the young man who is heir to the Churchill estates, and his feelings are further compounded when Frank takes off for London, merely to have a hair cut. However, Emma, despite knowing nothing about Frank Churchill is very taken with him and can't help but notice that most of his charm is directly aimed at her. The heroine finds herself flattered by Frank's attentions and engages in mild flirtation with him but she is less enthusiastic about the

Pickering.

Greatbatch.

EMMA.

There was no being displeased with such an encourager, for his admiration made him discern a likeness before it was possible.

CLASSIC LITERATURE

ABOVE Colour illustration depicting a scene from Jane Austen's novel *Emma*

arrival of Jane Fairfax, a beautiful and accomplished young woman of whom Emma is jealous.

Knightley is keen to support Jane and defends her from Emma claiming she deserves compassion. Unlike Emma, Jane will have to work as a governess in order to give herself some standing in the community and, as is typical of Austen, suspicion, misunderstandings and intrigue ensue. Mrs Weston suspects that Knightley is keen to involve himself with Jane romantically, however, Emma cannot entertain the idea. Tiring of Frank, Emma dismisses him from her mind as a potential suitor and believes he would be better suited to Harriet. Meanwhile, everyone else assumes that Emma and Frank are forming a close attachment. Next comes the village ball and Knightley gallantly offers to dance with Harriet who has just been completely humiliated by Elton and his new wife. The following day, Harriet is rescued once again when Frank saves her from gypsy beggars and she tells Emma that she has fallen in love with a man above her social station. Emma wrongly assumes that Harriet is talking about Frank Churchill and she laughs at Knightley's suggestion that Jane and Frank may have a secret understanding. At a picnic attended by Jane's aunt, Miss Bates – herself a kindly soul – Emma is less than kind to Jane's kin and openly flirts with Frank, an action for which she is pulled up short by Knightley. At the loss of her brother-in-law's approval Emma is reduced to tears.

News then arrives that Frank's frail aunt in London has died. But the news doesn't just affect Frank, it brings about an unexpected revelation that slowly begins to unravel all the suspicion and intrigue that abounded the community of Highbury. It transpires that Frank and Jane are secretly engaged and that his attentions towards Emma were a cover for his true feelings. With his uncle's approval, Frank is now free to marry Jane and Emma worries that Harriet will, once again, be humiliated. But Harriet surprises her friend by revealing that she is in love with Knightley – not Frank – and she strongly believes that her feelings are reciprocated. But, the news does not bring happiness for the heroine who has to admit to herself that she too is in love with George Knightley. Emma is placated when Knightley declares his love for her and Harriet is saved further upset and humiliation when Robert Martin proposes to her for a second time. The novel ends with two weddings and the answers to who loves whom.

Austen was wrongly convinced that, as the author, she would be one of the few people who would actually like the character of Emma. With her handsome looks and comfortable life, Austen warns the reader that her heroine is quite used to her own way and thinks "a little too much of herself". But, by using a narrator who comfortably slips between narrating the story and relating things from Emma's point of view, Austen is not clear about how harsh she wishes her readers to be in their opinions of Emma and, although the narration is quite complicated, can leave the reader feeling both sympathetic and frustrated by the main character.

CLASSIC LITERATURE

Persuasion (published posthumously 1818)

Although her health was failing, Austen wrote *Persuasion* in less than a year. But it would be another year after her death before the fifth manuscript would make it into print in 1818, published by John Murray. The book made a tidy profit of £500 – which doesn't seem much by today's standards – however, it was more money than Jane Austen would have seen in her lifetime.

Representing a mature style of writing, more so than any of the previous novels, the book is an exciting comic, yet satirical story, once again aimed at the echelons of the titled upper classes. However, Austen does reflect the esteem for which she, and society in general, had for the British Navy as defender of the British Empire. The navy heroes in the novel serve to introduce Austen's ideal of rougher manliness than the gentile landed gentry whom she so convincingly portrayed in the four earlier works, and *Northanger Abbey*, which was published in a bound volume with *Persuasion*. At 27, the protagonist, Anne Elliot, is no longer considered youthful. This was a first for Austen and perhaps marked her own feelings. However, the novel was also innovative in that it discussed the worth of the self-made man, in particular, Captain Frederick Wentworth. Austen was keen to discuss the worthiness of men who reached the upper echelons of society through their own initiative and not just because they were born to such standing.

Respected, titled landowners, the Elliots open the novel with a brief historical background. Lady Elliot had died 14 years previously and Sir Walter was left bringing up three daughters, Elizabeth and Anne, who are single, and Mary, the youngest who is married to wealthy Charles Musgrove. Sir Walter has growing

LEFT A television adaptation of *Persuasion* starring Rupert Penry-Jones as *Captain Wentworth*, and Sally Hawkins as *Anne Elliot*, 2007

debts brought about by his lavish spending but when family friend, Lady Russell, who acts as a mother figure in place of the late Lady Elliot, suggests that he curb his overspending he is mortified to learn that reducing his outgoings would mean giving up his comforts. As a vain man, Sir Walter is horrified, but faces no other option so the family relocate to Bath, where living expenses would be more manageable. Their former home, Kellynch Hall, the family estate, is promptly rented to Admiral and Mrs Croft, an exceptionally wealthy couple. Sir Walter is prejudiced in his belief that the navy can propel ordinary men into positions of

CLASSIC LITERATURE

distinction, however, he is satisfied that Admiral Croft is a suitable tenant for his home. Incidentally, Anne Elliot is desperately in love with Mrs Croft's brother. Eight years before, Anne was engaged to him and was persuaded to call off the union by Lady Russell – who did not deem the young man suitable by the nature of his more lowly birth. By meeting with Mrs Sophia Croft, Anne is hoping she will see Captain Frederick Wentworth once again.

Mrs Clay, a widow and lower class family friend, accompanies Sir Walter and Elizabeth to Bath while Anne decides to stay with Charles Musgrove and her sister Mary for a couple of months at Uppercross Cottage. Mary is prone to complaining and Anne finds herself listening sympathetically to her sister's woes. In fact, Charles Musgrove would have preferred to marry Anne (she refused him because of her continued love for Wentworth), but he remains patient to his wife's problems. Anne becomes involved with Charles's family and here she enjoys the company of Mr and Mrs Musgrove and their daughters, Henrietta and Louisa. The Musgrove's home at Uppercross is a functionally busy and loving household. The environment is good for Anne who feels she lacked a loving home with her father and older sister. Great excitement abounds when news is received that Captain Wentworth, who has just returned from sea, will be visiting his sister at Kellynch Hall. Musgrove and Wentworth soon become friends and the captain becomes a daily visitor at Uppercross where his manner towards Anne is conciliatory and polite, much to her disappointment. In fact, Wentworth seems rather taken with the Musgrove sisters, Henrietta, and particularly Louisa. Anne is sensible enough to keep her feelings to herself and resigns herself to the fact that she has lost her love forever.

The family take a trip to Lyme where Wentworth suggests that they visit his friends, the Harvilles. It is here that Anne comes to the attention of a gentleman named Mr Elliot. He is Anne's cousin and the heir to Kellynch Hall. While out walking one morning on the beach, Louisa Musgrove is knocked unconscious in a fall and it is Anne who remains calm and does all she can for her friend while everyone else believes the young woman to be dead. It is Anne who summons help for the injured Louisa, who although destined to recover, will need to spend some considerable time in Lyme. Wentworth blames himself for the accident and determines to help the Musgrove family. The accident has tempered Louisa's impetuous nature and she becomes acquainted with Captain James Benwick, a friend of the Harvilles, who is mourning the death of his fiancée and sister of his friend, Fanny Harville. Meanwhile, Anne returns to Uppercross to care for the younger Musgrove children but after a few weeks leaves to stay with trusted friend, Lady Russell.

Sometime after Christmas festivities, Anne and Lady Russell depart for Bath where they rejoin the Elliot household. Sir Walter and Elizabeth are glad to have

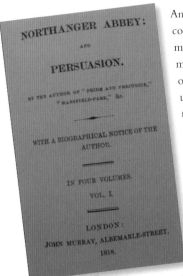

Anne to stay, which makes her more comfortable, as she was convinced that they cared little for her. Here, Anne is introduced more formally to her cousin, Mr William Elliot who has, by now, made peace with his estranged uncle, Sir Walter. The fall out occurred when Elliot married a woman whom Sir Walter deemed unsuitable for his nephew, but William is now a widower. Despite the heal in the family rift, Anne wonders what prompted her cousin to suddenly appear and make his apologies, however, she finds Elliot pleasing, although she remains wary of him. Elliot, it seems, wishes for Anne to become his wife. Meanwhile, she has also been reacquainted with Mrs Smith, her old school friend, and one-time close friend of Elliot, who has recently been widowed herself. Mrs Smith confides in Anne that Elliot only wants to marry her to ensure that he becomes sole heir to Kellynch Hall. She also warns the protagonist that she was treated badly by Anne's cousin in the past and that Elliot fears Sir Walter will marry Mrs Clay, and possibly have a son, which would end his right to inherit the family estate. Of course, Anne is appalled by this news. Mrs Clay, it is revealed, is in collusion with Elliot.

The Crofts also arrived in Bath and they bring the Elliots some news. Henrietta is engaged to be married to her cousin, Charles Hayter, while Louisa has agreed to marry Captain Benwick, the man she met while convalescing in Lyme. Anne is pleased for her friends and is particularly overjoyed that Captain Wentworth is not one of the betrothed. He too arrives in Bath and by now is exceedingly rich. Sir Walter reluctantly allows Wentworth to join the family's social circle. Wentworth, who has not lost his feelings for Anne – anymore than she has lost hers for him – becomes jealous when he believes that Elliot and Anne may be united and he writes his former love a letter in which he pours out his heart. Unsurprisingly, Anne is overjoyed at his declaration of undying love and they soon become engaged. With the increase in Wentworth's estate, this time both Sir Walter and Lady Russell give the couple their blessing. Elliot is shocked that his plans have been foiled and when he leaves Bath with Mrs Clay the rumours are rife that they are together. This just confirms for Anne that they were in it together all along.

The novel's protagonist, Anne Elliot is a practical woman who is often overlooked by her father, yet remains conscious of her duty to her social position and manages to balance what is expected of her against her own desires. However, with Captain Wentworth having made his own fortune by making his way up the naval ranks, he is deemed unsuitable for Anne by Sir Walter, despite his kind and gentle nature, his virtue and his good education. Like all Austen novels, Sir Walter is taken on a journey of learning and acceptance and eventually, when Wentworth is proved to be a suitable match for his daughter he relents and gives his blessing. Interestingly, at the end of the novel, only Elizabeth Elliot remains unmarried. As a vain woman who places great emphasis on social standing, she has decided that there is no suitor of adequate birth and so prefers to miss out on the happiness of love. In classic Austen style, some characters have been rewarded for their honest and virtuous approach to life, others have learned a great deal and some have not changed their stance at all. It is novels such as *Persuasion* that show how clearly perceptive Austen actually was with regard to human nature and how much she was encouraging society to think and re-evaluate its perceptions and overriding principles.

Northanger Abbey (published posthumously in 1818)

The novel was actually the first ready for publication, even though work on *Sense And Sensibility* and *Pride And Prejudice* had already begun. *Northanger Abbey* was written in 1789 and revised for publication in 1803 and sold to Crosbie & Co in London. However, it remained at the publishers for many years on the shelves and was eventually sold back to Henry Austen for £10 – the same amount for which it was bought – although to be fair to Crosbie & Co they had no idea that the author was Jane Austen who had already published four popular novels. It was further revised before being bound with *Persuasion* and published posthumously in late December 1817, although the title page records the date of publication as 1818. It was the first two volumes of what was intended to be a four-volume set. Originally entitled *Susan* after the main character in the novel, *Northanger Abbey* was written at a time of great political turmoil at the turn of the century when often, government censorship was rife in the literary world.

When *Susan* was eventually renamed, Austen also chose to change the name of her protagonist to Catherine. Perhaps not as acutely executed in terms of ironic wit and satire as her later novels, *Northanger Abbey* is undoubtedly Austen in its approach, and the irony is often exaggerated and almost becomes sarcastic. It is generally an ironic parody of Gothic novels – popular at the time when Jane was writing – and the new and upcoming light romances that were gaining in momentum, despite their unsophisticated approach in early modern literature.

Northanger Abbey is the story of young Catherine Morland who is coming of age. The novel is divided into two sections: Book I and Book II. Both in setting and

LEFT Scene from a
television adaption of
Northanger Abbey, 2007

tone the books are significantly different. In Book I, the Allen family, who are friends of the Morlands, offer to take Catherine with them to Bath where wealthier members of British society abide. An eager, 17-year-old Catherine accepts the invitation leaving her relatively sheltered life for an exciting new world. Here she

CLASSIC LITERATURE

ABOVE *Northanger Abbey*, novel

RIGHT Scene from the *Northanger Abbey* television adaption, 2007

meets Henry Tilney, a young clergyman who impresses the youngster with his wit and conversation and she quickly falls for him, despite not seeing him again for some time after their initial meeting. Mrs Thorpe, an old acquaintance of Mrs Allen, has three daughters. Isabella Thorpe is slightly older than Catherine and introduces her new friend to the social circles in Bath where they attend balls, dances and engage in fashion and gossip. Both the girls' brothers, James Morland and John Thorpe then come to the city – the two men were friends at Oxford University – and Isabella wastes no time in making her feelings for James Morland obvious through her flirtatious advances. The couple fall in love and everyone is aware of it, except Catherine.

John Thorpe, in turn, attempts to woo Catherine, but a chance meeting at a dance with Henry Tilney puts paid to his romantic ambitions. Isabella is no longer much available as a companion for Catherine and she turns to Eleanor Tilney, Henry's sister for friendship. Eleanor establishes in her own mind that her new friend has feelings for Henry but keeps her thoughts to herself.

When rain washes away Catherine's chances of taking a walk with Eleanor and Henry she finds herself pressured into riding with John Thorpe. During the ride she spots the brother and sister heading for her house for the planned walk, but John angers Catherine when he refuses to let her stop and inform her friends that she is unavailable. Later, she is able to apologise to them and the three make plans for another walk. But, once again, John, James and Isabella interrupt their plans and pressure her into another outing. But this time, Catherine refuses and takes her longed-for walk with Henry and his sister around Beechen Cliff. Catherine is pleased when she discovers that both Eleanor and Henry share her love of books

CLASSIC LITERATURE

and novels. She returns home later to find her brother has become engaged to Isabella Thorpe. She briefly meets with John Thorpe who is leaving Bath for a short period, however, unbeknown to Catherine he believes that she is in love with him.

The second book begins with the arrival of Captain Frederick Tilney, older brother of Henry and Eleanor. He and Isabella (who by now is not impressed with James Morland's modest income) begin a dangerous flirtation while Eleanor invites Catherine to her family home in Northanger Abbey. General Tilney, Eleanor's father, is also pleased to invite his daughter's young friend to his home and Catherine, once again, eagerly accepts the invitation. She is particularly taken with the idea of visiting a real abbey and hoping to see more of Henry, but before she leaves, Isabella informs her that John is intending to propose. Catherine asks her friend to write to her brother and apologise on her behalf that any proposal from John would be refused. Frederick Tilney and Isabella then openly flirt in front of Catherine who is appalled by their behaviour. She immediately asks Henry to make sure that Frederick leaves Isabella alone for the sake of her relationship with James, however, Henry refuses. He is well aware that Isabella is just as guilty as Frederick, but hopes that the news that his brother's regiment will be leaving Bath shortly will be enough to placate Catherine.

The protagonist is so intrigued by Northanger Abbey on her journey there that she tells Henry what she imagines it will be like. She concludes that she thinks it will resemble the haunted ruins of the Gothic novels she loves, and Henry is so amused at her thoughts that he tells Catherine about how her first night there might be in a hypothetical account which includes storms, secret passages and mysterious goings-on. By comparison, the abbey turns out to be duller than Catherine expected and all her frightening ideas about what it should be like are abruptly shattered. In fact, disappointingly for Catherine, the abbey is a normal family home. While at the abbey, with an overactive imagination, Catherine becomes intrigued over the death of General Tilney's wife some years before. With her mind on Gothic plots she even imagines that the General murdered his wife and she sneaks into Mrs Tilney's old quarters where, unsurprisingly, she discovers absolutely nothing out of the ordinary. But, Catherine is caught by Henry who guesses her motives for being in his mother's old room. He mortifies and shames his house guest who immediately resumes her moralistic behaviour in order to win back his approval.

James Morland writes to Catherine to inform her that his engagement to Isabella has been called off and she immediately blames Frederick for the break up. However, Henry tells her of Isabella's part in proceedings and she becomes convinced of her friend's guilt. Henry takes Catherine to visit his house at

Woodston and the General begins to hint at marriage between the young couple. A second letter arrives for Catherine. This time it's from Isabella asking her to apologise to James on her behalf. It seems that Frederick Tilney has left her. Understandably, Catherine is offended and angry that Isabella is trying to manipulate her. Henry leaves for his house in Woodston and the General travels away on business. But he returns unexpectedly and demands that Eleanor send Catherine away from Northanger Abbey the following day. Although embarrassed, Eleanor carries out her father's wishes and Catherine has no choice but to return to Fullerton, her family home.

As glad as her family are to see Catherine, they are annoyed by General Tilney's rude treatment of their daughter and she, in turn, becomes depressed. However, Henry suddenly arrives at Fullerton and proposes to Catherine explaining that John Thorpe was the man behind his father's sudden dismissal of her. John had told the General that Catherine was from a wealthy family (at the time when he thought she

ABOVE & RIGHT
Scenes from the
Northanger Abbey
television adaption,
2007

CLASSIC LITERATURE

loved him), but he became bitter when he learned that she did not in fact love him and spitefully told General Tilney that the Morlands were virtually impoverished. Eleanor's father was devastated by John Thorpe's news, but was in a more jovial mood when his daughter soon after married a wealthy man. Once he is correctly informed that the Morlands have a modest income he relents and consents to the marriage of Henry and Catherine.

There are several Gothic novels mentioned in *Northanger Abbey*, including two by Neo-classical author, Anne Radcliffe: *The Mysteries of Udolpho* and *The Italian*. Austen uses satire to bring the earlier novelists' books into her own and repeats this exercise with Regina Maria Roche's *Clermont*. When later research revealed that these novels actually did exist there was a move to publish them despite the fact that Austen had used them in parody. Austen's biographer, Claire Tomalin, has suggested that Jane intended this light-hearted parody, containing references to well-known literature of the time, as entertainment to be enjoyed by her family.

CLASSIC LITERATURE

Juvenilia, short stories and unfinished novels

Interestingly, Austen was exploring her chosen subject matter right from the start of her writing career. *The Three Sisters,* written around 1792 is written as a short epistolary novel – meaning the story is told through a series of letters written by the main characters – in much the same way as Samuel Richardson's *Pamela.* Even though it is early Austen, it too, already contains much of the irony that was to become her trademark and implicitly criticises the social expectations that women may only progress in life if they climb the social ladder through marriage. However, despite the fact that Austen's juvenilia and later novels all contain this concept she herself didn't believe that women should have to marry in order to leave the parental home or save themselves from abject poverty.

What seems incredible about Austen's insight is that she was just 17 when she wrote *The Three Sisters* and was just coming of marrying age herself. In the short novel, it is the character of Sophie who represents Austen's own views and not Mary, who is shown to have a weak disposition, and who makes an inappropriate decision which the author harshly exposes. However, Austen is careful not to minimise the pressures that women were facing at the time. Other juvenilia includes *Love And Freindship* with its famous mis-spelling, *History Of England, Catherine, The Beautiful Cassandra* which was one of the funniest works ever written by Austen, about her sister Cassandra and dedicated (with permission) to her life-long companion and confident, *Jack And Alice* and *Frederic And Elfrida.*

Along with short works, Austen also wrote three unfinished novels. *The Watsons* was eventually completed by Jane Austen's niece Catherine Hubback, however, it

LEFT Jane wrote about the social pretensions of her time

CLASSIC LITERATURE

was probably *Sanditon* that was the most important. Written while she was ill in 1817, the novel is also known as *Sand And Sanditon* and was originally entitled *The Brothers*. Here, the author explores her interest in social politics. In it, the residents of Sanditon must create a town within their own social circles and the town is built around the words of the inhabitants and the conversations that they have rather than through the practical construction of homes and buildings. Based around the Parker brothers – for whom it was presumably originally named – the author shows her interest in communication; something she had experimented with since her first unfinished work, *Lady Susan*.

Despite the fact that Austen had less than six months to live when she began the novel, it is fresh, innovative and extremely witty and builds on the theme set out in *Persuasion* that men of lowly birth can, and do, overcome prejudice to acquire the status, through sheer hard work and determination, that puts them squarely in the upper echelons of society. Many have tried to continue the manuscript in the style of Austen with what they see as her vision. Some such authors include Marie Dobbs and Anne Telscombe, (suspected pseudonyms either for one or the other, or perhaps pseudonyms for the same person) D J Eden and a version entitled *Jane Austen's Sanditon; A Continuation* by Anna Austen Lefroy, the author's niece.

Lady Susan, written around 1795, shows Austen's epistolary genre at its best and it seems a shame it remained unpublished. The short novel begins with the selfish behaviour of Lady Susan, a woman who is resigned to finding a husband for herself and her daughter but who enjoys plenty of dalliances on her quest. The characters are manifested by their actions as a result of the letters they receive while the heroine alters the tone of her own letters depending on the recipient. One thing is clear, there are many letters between the female characters that portray feminine gossip and jealousy. *The Watsons,* which remained incomplete, was written around 1803 and it was probably abandoned when her father died in Bath in 1805. The story centres around Mr Watson, a widowed clergyman who is gravely ill at the start of the novel, and who has two sons and four daughters. His youngest child, Emma, has been more fortunate than her siblings and was brought up by a wealthy aunt who gave her a grounded education and more genteel environment in which to grow. When her aunt remarries, Emma finds she has to return to her father where she is astonished by the reckless way in which two of her older sisters are trying to find themselves husbands. Living nearby is the titled Osborne family and Emma soon attracts the attention of young Lord Osborne. Ultimately, Emma rejects social position, and to some extent duty, when she decides to marry the Osborne's young tutor. At least two attempts were made to complete the novel. One during the 19th century by one of Austen's nieces, the other was simply written under the name of "Another Lady". However, it was Catherine Hubback who eventually completed her aunt's work in the mid 19th century.

CLASSIC LITERATURE

Chapter 3

Film and Television

All six of Austen's major novels have been adapted for the cinema and small screen to varying degrees of success.

Sense And Sensibility

RIGHT On the set of the film *Sense and Sensibility*, 1995

In 1995, *Sense And Sensibility* was adapted for the big screen by renowned actress Emma Thompson and the feature was directed by the highly talented Ang Lee. Filmed on location in Devon, including the cobbled streets of Plymouth and at Saltram House, Berry Pomeroy and Compton Castle, the adaptation is particularly faithful to the novel. Released in the US in December 1995 and the UK in February 1996, the film won a number of awards including the Academy award for Best Adapted Screenplay (Emma Thompson) and the Golden Bear award for Best Film at the Berlin International Film Festival. BAFTA awards included Best Film (Lindsay Doran and Ang Lee), Best Performance by an Actress in a Leading Role (Emma Thompson) and Best Performance by an Actress in a Supporting Role (Kate Winslet). Other cast members include Hugh Grant as Edward Ferrars, Robert Hardy as Sir John Middleton, Alan Rickman as Colonel Brandon, Imelda Staunton as Charlotte Palmer, Imogen Stubbs as Lucy Steele and Hugh Laurie as Mr Palmer.

CLASSIC LITERATURE

Pride And Prejudice

Ten years after the film debut of *Sense And Sensibility, Pride And Prejudice* – starring Keira Knightley (as Elizabeth Bennet), Matthew Macfadyen, Brenda Blethyn and Donald Sutherland – was released in the UK in September 2005. Based on the screenplay by Deborah Moggach, the film was directed by Joe Wright and filmed on location around the UK, including the stately Chatsworth House in Derbyshire and Wilton House in Salisbury which was used to represent Pemberley. Groombridge Place in Kent was used as a location for Longbourn while Basildon Park in Berkshire represented Netherfield Park. Burghley, near Stamford in Lincolnshire, and the town itself, were also used during filming.

As is customary when a comprehensive work of literature is adapted into around two hours of film, there were differences between the film and the original story, where cuts needed to be made. For instance, here, several supporting characters were eliminated from the screenplay and the crisis endured by the Bennet family when Lydia elopes with Wickham is compressed. Nominated for five BAFTA awards, the film won the Carl Foreman Award for Most Promising newcomer (Joe Wright, Director). Dame Judi Dench and Penelope Wilton also starred in this timeless classic.

But the film was not the only adaptation to hit the screen. Ten years earlier, the BBC featured a television adaptation in six episodes shown between September and October 1995. Starring Colin Firth as Darcy – a role for which he will never be forgotten – and Jennifer Ehle as Lizzy Bennet, the production featured supporting roles from Alison Steadman (as the hapless Mrs Bennet), Crispin Bonham-Carter (Mr Bingley) and Anna Chancellor as his spiteful manipulative sister (Miss Bingley) as well as Susannah Harker, Julia Sawalha (who played Lydia), David Bamber (as Mr Collins), Adrian Lukis and Benjamin Whitrow.

LEFT Joe Wright poses for photographs after winning the Carl Foreman award for *Pride and Prejudice*

CLASSIC LITERATURE

Mansfield Park

In 1999, the UK film, *Mansfield Park,* was released. Loosely based on Austen's novel of the same name and written and directed by Patricia Rozema, the majority of the film was shot on location in Kirby Hall and starred Frances O'Connor and Jonny Lee Miller. It debuted at the Montreal Film Festival on 27 August that same year

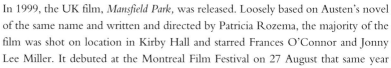

and also starred Harold Pinter, Lindsay Duncan, Sheila Gish and Hannah Taylor Gordon as a young Fanny Price. Then in 2007, ITV brought out a television adaptation starring Billie Piper. The series debuted on Sunday 18 March, but received some criticism for changing too many scenes from the book for the small screen and for not staying true to Austen's original work.

Emma

The period film, *Emma*, was released on 2 August 1996 and starred Gwyneth Paltrow in the leading role. Directed by Douglas McGrath and also starring Jeremy Northam, Toni Collette, Greta Scacchi, Juliet Stevenson and Ewan McGregor, the film gained rave reviews while Paltrow won critical acclaim for her portrayal of Emma. Comic scenes were provided by Alan Cumming and Juliet Stevenson as Mr and Mrs

Elton while real-life mother and daughter Phyllida Law and Sophie Thompson played the roles of Mrs Bates and Miss Bates. However, the film faced competition from the television movie that was released the same year in November.

Adapted by Andrew Davies and directed by Diarmuid Lawrence, the television movie also won critical acclaim and went on to receive two coveted Emmys. Starring Kate Beckinsale as Emma, Mark Strong as Mr Knightley and Prunella Scales as Miss Bates, many critics felt that this version was more true to Austen's original work and that generally the screenplay production was superior to the more glamorous film version. All critics seem to agree that Paltrow and Beckinsale are well cast as Emma – both are good – but the production of the later version just tips the balance for many.

The fact that both came out at roughly the same time caused some confusion, and, whereas Sophie Thompson's interpretation of Miss Bates in the film version was classed by many critics as outstanding, there was a general consensus that the casting of Prunella Scales in the same role for the ITV version was a little odd – even though the actress gave a great performance.

CLASSIC LITERATURE

Persuasion

In 1995 the BBC released a television film version of *Persuasion* starring Amanda Root as Anne Elliot and Ciaran Hinds as Captain Frederick Wentworth. Other cast members included Susan Fleetwood as Lady Russell, Corin Redgrave as Sir Walter Elliot and Fiona Shaw as Mrs Croft. Samuel West took the role of estranged nephew, William Elliot while Sophie Thompson was a convincing Mary Musgrove. Elizabeth Elliot was played by Phoebe Nicholls and the adaptation was directed by Roger Michell with a screenplay by Nick Dear. The film was a resounding success and won BAFTA awards for Best Single Drama, Best Photography and Lighting, Best Costume Design, Best Design and Best Original Television Music.

It was followed by another television adaptation in 2007 starring Sally Hawkins, Rupert Penry-Jones, Alice Krige, Anthony Head, Julia Davis and Mary Stockley. Directed by Adrian Shergold and adapted by Simon Burke, the production wasn't deemed to have made the dizzy heights of its predecessor although Tobias Menzies who played William Elliot received rave reviews.

Northanger Abbey

The first of Austen's novels was adapted for the small screen in 1986 by A&E Network and the BBC. Directed by Giles Foster with a screenplay by Maggie Wadey, the cast starred Katharine Schlesinger as Catherine and Peter Firth as Henry Tilney. Supporting roles were given by Robert Hardy (General Tilney), Googie Withers (Mrs Allen), Cassie Stuart (Isabella Thorpe), Jonathan Coy (John Thorpe), Philip Bird (James Morland), Ingrid Lacey (Eleanor Tilney) and Greg Hicks (Frederick Tilney).

LEFT *Persuasion* won
five BAFTAS

Chapter 4

Celebrating Jane Austen

Jane Austen's House Museum

The Jane Austen's House Museum is Austen's former home, at Chawton, where she wrote some of her best works and is today preserved for her thousands of fans the world over. Open all year round (although weekends only apply during January and February – it is also shut on 25 and 26 December), the former home of this popular novelist offers a great deal to those who visit.

Bought by Mr T Edward Carpenter in 1947 with additional funding from the Jane Austen Society, Austen's former home was turned into an independent charity which is administered by the Jane Austen Memorial Trust. Established by Edward Carpenter, among others, the Memorial Trust has run the Jane Austen's House Museum in the author's memory ever since its inception and as a self-supporting charity relies on admission charges, sales from the shop as well as grants and donations. The aims of the Memorial Trust are to preserve the museum for the nation and to acquire, catalogue and conserve the museum's collection of artefacts

LEFT The Jane Austen
House museum

as well as interpreting Austen's life for those who visit. As well as the extensive education programme, the Jane Austen's House Museum also aims to develop its role and facilities to meet the demands of visitors to the museum and those who make enquiries about Jane Austen across the globe.

It was here that Austen spent the last eight years of her life where she revised *Sense And Sensibility*, *Pride And Prejudice* and *Northanger Abbey* and where she wrote *Emma*, *Persuasion* and *Mansfield Park*. Despite the fact that the house is now essentially a museum, it retains the charm of a family home, where the 17th century building tells

CLASSIC LITERATURE

the story of Austen and her family through its rooms, exhibition and artefacts. The museum offers substantial assistance to those visitors in need of wheelchair access or those with impaired vision and even houses a reference library which includes the various editions of Austen's published novels as well as other books and titles to help those who wish to study the author in greater depth. The library also has a collection of translations of Austen titles.

As a result of the educational work carried out by the Jane Austen's House Museum and the Chawton House Library, they have received the Sandford Award for their study linked to the schools curriculum and beyond.

As well as providing an educative environment, the museum also strives to promote Jane Austen and it carries out this work by holding special events. In December 2007, the museum gave a two-day exhibition with explanations given by Mr Samuel Adams on how the festive season would have been celebrated in the Georgian and Regency periods. The topics covered included customs, practices and traditions that Austen herself would have experienced. The museum also offers a comprehensive service for schools, and works together with Chawton House Library to educate those pupils in primary and secondary education. All key stages are catered for while the shop provides visitors with a myriad of books and souvenirs for purchase. It is the best bookshop in the UK for Jane Austen titles and helpful staff is on hand to advise customers. It is possible to buy Jane Austen Society publications, Jane Austen letters, Jane Austen sayings books, local interest and history books, novels, study books, critiques, biographies and family histories as well as children's books relating to Jane Austen and activity books for younger readers.

The shop also sells linen, china, postcards, greetings cards, stationery, quill pens and calligraphy sets (with ink) as well as many other souvenirs. A catalogue of items contained in the shop is also available.

LEFT A costume designed by John Bright and Jenny Beavan for "*Sense and Sensibility*" is displayed at the Academy of Motion Picture Arts & Sciences

CLASSIC LITERATURE

RIGHT The Jane
Austen Centre, Bath

For further information contact:

Jane Austen's House Museum

Chawton

Alton

Hampshire

GU34 1SD

Tel: +44 (0)1420 832 262

The Jane Austen Centre

The Jane Austen Centre in Bath is much more than a centre in the town where the famous author once lived. The website alone provides an online magazine featuring more than 500 articles, an online gift shop as well as information about the Jane Austen Festival, walking tours, an online quiz, the Jane Austen's Regency World magazine and a monthly E-newsletter which keeps fans up-to-date with relevant news and views. The permanent exhibition at the Jane Austen Centre tells the story of the author's experiences in Bath and the effect that living there had on the novelist, as well as the influences the city had on her writings, particularly with regard to *Northanger Abbey* and *Persuasion,* both of which were set partly in the city.

The exhibition at the centre was created with the help and guidance of the Jane Austen Society and other leading experts. During 2007, the centre was fortunate to acquire the costumes from ITV's adaptation of *Persuasion* which won designer, Andrea Galer, a BAFTA for Best Costume Design. Set in a Georgian house in the centre of Bath, the centre is run by Director, David Baldock and, like the Jane Austen's House Museum, created something special for Christmas festivities in 2007 when they housed a special exhibition illustrating celebrations as Jane Austen would

CLASSIC LITERATURE

have experienced them. A special feature at the centre was the Queen Charlotte Christmas Tree – a Regency invention which was first introduced in England in 1800 by the wife of King George III.

In an exciting and interesting, if somewhat cheeky experiment, Jane Austen's *Regency World* magazine decided to send sample chapters of *Pride And Prejudice*, *Northanger Abbey* and *Persuasion* out to roughly 18 publishing houses and literary agents to see how a Jane Austen novel would have fared in today's cut-throat publishing environment. Not very well as it turns out. Sent with a brief synopsis and the biographical details of "Alison Laydee", a pun on "A Lady" the name under which Austen herself published her novels, the chapters were rejected by all but one recipient who recognised that the sample manuscripts were possibly by Austen. As

Pride And Prejudice has been voted the "number one book that the British nation could not live without" it seems sad that major players in the publishing world couldn't recognise a masterpiece when they saw one or didn't realise the significance of what they'd received. The article's author, David Lassman was staggered by the response he received which consisted of firm, but polite, no thank-you letters.

The centre also offers varied entertainment. "Lecture and Lunch Series" are held midweek where a buffet lunch follows a lecture at a very reasonable price. The centre strives to improve its facilities and the exhibitions it offers, and one of its attractions is its Walking Tours which are well worth it considering that Bath is one of only three World Heritage Cities. The tours take visitors around the city to visit the houses where Jane Austen lived as well as the settings for the novels *Northanger Abbey* and *Persuasion*. Walks start at 11.00am and last an hour and a half while during the summer months of July and August walking tours are also given on Friday and Saturday evenings at 6.00pm.

Group visits for both schools and others are also available and visits are tailored to the individual needs of each group. Adult groups enjoy an introductory talk by an experienced guide (most staff are former teachers) in a classical Georgian room before being shown to the Jane Austen exhibition where visitors are invited to wander at their leisure. Guides are on hand to answer any Austen related queries or to give historical information about Bath. And, visitors are welcome to visit the Regency Tea Rooms which offer home made cakes, light snakes and real leaf tea. The centre is happy to accommodate groups in tailor-made tours and will gladly arrange for a particular group to take a guided tour of Bath before concluding their visit at the centre and the Tea Rooms. The centre will even work around groups outside normal opening hours if arranged in advance where visitors can gain exclusive access to the Jane Austen Centre.

CLASSIC LITERATURE

RIGHT Bath Abbey an example of the stunning Architecture on show in Bath

The Jane Austen Festival is held in Bath in the autumn each year and in 2008 the dates set for this prestigious event are 19 to 28 September, run by Festival Director, David Lassman and his team. The aims of the festival are to provide a number of events suitable for all those interested in Jane Austen and the Regency era. Preparations for the 2008 festival are currently underway and tickets for the Jane Austen Festival Regency Ball are already on sale. Other highlights include Europe's largest Regency Promenade which comprises a large number of people dressing in Regency costumes while walking the grand terraces of Bath accompanied by dancing and music, as well as the dance workshop held in the Assembly Rooms and the Jane Austen Day celebrations. There are also mystery drama tours, walking tours and lectures, music, film and special guests. For all those interested in Jane Austen and Bath the festival is a must see.

The Jane Austen Centre Online Magazine is updated monthly with articles covering the aspects of Austen's life and the Regency era. The magazine covers Regency fashion, recipes, historical information and articles on Austen's work and how her writing influences and affects people today. There are also media reviews on the latest films, sequels and television adaptations as well as biographies of people from the Regency period – a Who's Who. The online magazine also has a novella, *There Must be Murder,* the sequel to *Northanger Abbey*, which is published monthly by chapter.

For further information contact:
The Jane Austen Centre
40 Gay Street
Queens Square
Bath
BA1 2NT
Tel: +44 (0)1225 443000

CLASSIC LITERATURE

The Jane Austen Society

There are many Jane Austen societies found throughout the world.

Australasia

The Jane Austen Society of Australia (JASA) was founded in 1989 by Nora Walker for the benefit of those living in the southern hemisphere to be able to celebrate this extraordinary author. The JASA prides itself on not being stuffy, and invites scholars, amateurs, professionals and enthusiasts to gather together to study and appreciate the genius that was surely Jane Austen. The society is interested in her life and times, as well as her works, and believes firmly that Jane's environment contributed greatly to her writing. The society also focuses on the fact that the author's interests were unlimited and as a result they claim that so are theirs. Meetings for members take place every two months and conferences and workshops are also held on a regular basis. A JASA party is held in December each year to celebrate Austen's birthday. *Sensibilities* is the bi-annual publication which members receive as part of their membership package.

With a membership of around 450 members, the society today has independent groups in Sidney, Melbourne and Adelaide.

Europe

The Jane Austen Society in the UK is headed by President Richard Knight. Founded in 1940 by Dorothy Darnell – who had the initial idea for a society – to help secure the cottage at Chawton where Austen spent the remainder of her days, the society aims to promote Jane Austen and interest in her life and works. The society's annual general

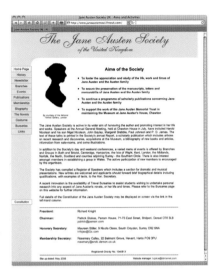

ABOVE Jane Austen Society website

meeting is held at Chawton House and invited speakers give an address to members which is then published in the annual report. There are historical notes and articles as well as an annual bibliography of Jane Austen's books, articles, book reviews and short notices while an annual newsletter includes a diary of events. The society is comprised of independent regional groups who are active in Bath and Bristol, Cambridge, Hampshire, Kent, London, the Midlands, Norfolk and the Isle of Wight. The society also runs charitable activities which include events such as the restoration of the Reverend George Austen's tombstone at St Swithin's Walcot Church in Bath. Costing roughly the same as membership in Australia and North America, membership of the UK society is £15 annually (although those overseas wishing to join the society pay an extra fee of £3.00) and life membership is offered at £250.

CLASSIC LITERATURE

North America

The Jane Austen Society of North America (JASNA) has a mission to foster the study, appreciation and understanding of Jane Austen's works, her life and times and her sheer genius. The society provides benefits for its members through grants and other funding which seeks to broaden knowledge. The society has an annual journal, entitled, *Persuasion* and publishes a newsletter, *JASNA News*, and also provides members with the opportunity to participate in regional groups across the US and Canada.

ABOVE Jane Austen Society website of North America

RIGHT Screenwriters and actors at the Jane Austen masterpiece theatre

The society also holds an annual meeting (over a weekend) which is held in a different location each year to maximise the numbers of members able to attend. This particular society prides itself on providing a "fun" environment for its members – it is keen to emphasise that Jane Austen was a comic writer. The society is pleased to offer membership to people from all walks of life. The society was founded by Canadian born, Joan Austen-Leigh, the great-great-great niece of the novelist and Jack Grey from New York, and came about when the two met at Chawton in 1975. Today, the society has more than 4,500 members.

South America

The Jane Austen Society of Buenos Aires is the only society in South America and is immensely proud of that fact. During its first three years, all members of the society re-read the six major novels and the three unfinished titles as well as

enjoying the BBC adaptations on video! The society was founded by Patrick Orpen Dudgeon in August 1997.

Other societies

There are also Jane Austen Societies in Scandinavia, Central Africa, Malaysia and the Netherlands. Interestingly, despite Jane Austen being well read in Asia, there are no societies in countries such as Japan and China to celebrate her life and works.

With her shrewd understanding of the human mind and infamous ironic wit, it is little wonder that Jane Austen is as much admired and revered for her works that resonate just as strongly with readers today, if not more so, than they did in the early 19th century.

CLASSIC LITERATURE

ALSO AVAILABLE:

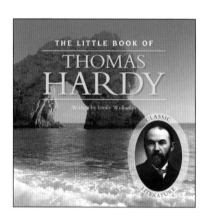

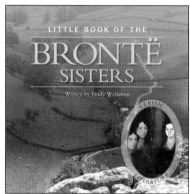

Available from all major stockists

The pictures in this book were provided courtesy of the following:

GETTY IMAGES
101 Bayham Street, London NW1 0AG

SHUTTERSTOCK
www.shutterstock.com

Creative Director: Kevin Gardner

Design and Artwork: David Wildish

Picture research: Ellie Charleston

Published by Green Umbrella Publishing

Publishers: Jules Gammond and Vanessa Gardner

Written by Emily Wollaston

CLASSIC LITERATURE